Everything to God in Prayer

Praying Daily with Purpose and Passion

By Terri Blazell-Wayson

© Copyright 2025 Terri Blazell-Wayson
All rights reserved.
Printed in the United States of America

Scripture quotations taken from The Holy Bible, New International Version®, NIV®. Copyright © 1973, 1978, 1984, 2011 by Biblica, Inc. Used with permission of Zondervan. All rights reserved worldwide.
www.zondervan.com

Acknowledgements

Thank you to my beloved friends who have prayed me through so many things. Those who encourage me and are always there for me. You know who you are.

Thank you to my Heavenly Father and to my Savior, Jesus who redeemed me.

Introduction

Does your prayer life frustrate you? Do you bounce between thundering Heaven's gates to silent discouragement? Is it monotonously repetitious or sporadic and incomplete? My prayer life has been all of these things.

I struggled with why I should pray, how I should pray and what I should pray about. A friend shared with me that she thought prayer was more about developing our character than about God answering them. But when Elijah called down fire from Heaven so severe it devoured a sacrifice, evaporated gallons of water and turned piles of rocks into charcoal, I don't think Elijah was just developing his character. He called out to God and God answered him.[1]

---

[1] I Kings 18

Study the life of any effective Christian and you will find someone whose life is centered on prayer. God doesn't just act when we pray; God acts because we pray.

Prayer should be a time of worship, meditation, adoration, reflection, confession and supplication. But how do we go about that?

This book is a thirty-one day daily prayer devotional that emphasizes the names and character of God and His son Jesus Christ. It will take you through the many aspects of prayer from praise to pouring out your heart one day at a time.

There are many books written about prayer and they are good books. But many of them have you reading about prayer. The idea of this book is to have you praying right from the start.

Almost every Christian knows that an effective prayer life should be a part of their Christian walk. But when it comes to "talking with God" the big question becomes "What do we talk about?"

Many times when I have started to pray, I would jump right into all the things I wanted God to change or fix or provide. But I wanted my prayer life to be about more than just asking for things. I wanted it to be fervent, passionate and meaningful.

Many years ago, someone shared with me the ACTS method of praying. If you are not familiar with it, ACTS is an acronym for:

>A = Adoration
>C = Confession
>T = Thanksgiving
>S = Supplication

A similar acronym is PRAY:

>P = Praise
>R = Repent
>A = Ask
>Y = Yield

These guides can help us pray with more focus and expand our prayer life to more than just asking God for things we want or need.

When Jesus disciples asked Him to teach them how to pray, Jesus taught them what is now called the Lord's Prayer[2]. It has similar steps as the prompts above but without a fancy acronym.

"Our Father in heaven, hallowed be your name."

Acknowledge who God is with worship and praise.

"Your kingdom come, your will be done."

Seek God's will above all else.

"Give us today our daily bread."

Come to Him with your needs.

"And forgive our debts, as we also have forgiven our debtors"

Grant forgiveness. Seek forgiveness.

"And lead us not into temptation but deliver us from the evil one."

Prayer for protection. I cannot do it alone.

The Lord's prayer can be repeated as is but I believe Jesus intended it to be more of an outline and we fill in the rest.

---

[2] Matthew 6:9-13

The premise is that before we come to God with our requests (supplication), we need to spend time in recognizing Him, worshipping Him, confessing our sins and thanking Him for what He has already done. The Lord's Prayer and the other acronyms above helped to give my prayers a blueprint. Like the foundation of a house, it provided a structure. To this structure, I made a list of people and things I wanted to pray for.

I prayed the list every day. As time went by, I felt that I was reciting the list more than I was engaging in the God of Heaven and the Creator of the universe. When someone shared a prayer need with me, I would add them to my list and my list got longer. Or I would promise to pray for them but in the busy-ness of everyday life often forgot. If I didn't pray the list, I felt guilty that I might be letting someone or Someone down as though failing to mention a name everyday may be the cause of any misfortune that came their way. Those farther down on the list were often short-changed as I either raced through them or stopped before even finishing.

My prayer life felt repetitious. Prayer became a heavy burden -not what God intended. Eventually I divided my list into seven columns; one for every day of the week. I was able to spend more time praying for each individual person on the now much shorter lists. I could take my time and pray for more people with more meaning. I even added an eighth column for those I do want to pray for every day. I've duplicated this chart at the back of the book for you to use in the same way.

When I met friends, I could honestly say, "I prayed for you this week." I'm still amazed at the response I get from that simple phrase. Sometimes it brings tears to both of our eyes. It reminds me of Matthew 6:8 where Jesus says our Heavenly Father knows our needs before we ask him. Praying weekly for my friends allows me to be on the giving end of that verse – sometimes we NEED someone praying for us as dearly as we need material things. I may not have known that they needed prayer or known what to specifically pray for but I was still praying for them when they needed it. How wonderful to know that God used me to fill that need for another before they even asked for it.

But there was still something missing. I didn't want my prayer life to just be about what I want or what I need. And it wasn't about what my friends wanted or my friends needed. God is not Santa Claus and I didn't want my prayers to be a "gimme this and fix that" list.

God is our Husband[3]. We are His bride. There is intimacy between a husband and wife. That is prayer. The intimacy of admiring and speaking words of love to your Beloved. Of breathing in His fragrance. Of spiritually resting in His arms. That is prayer.

---

[3] Isaiah 54:5

During my Bible readings, I often came across verses that reflected my prayers. Verses about who God is. Verses for praising Him. Verses about confession. I began writing them down and praying through some of these verses each day. Then I began organizing the verses into themes centered on the names of God such as Shepherd, Father, King. My simple prayer list grew into a prayer devotional. My prayer life became richer and my prayers more meaningful. I wasn't just reciting a list, I was actively talking to and worshipping God through His own God-breathed Word.

Eventually, it became the start of what is now this book; a daily devotion that can be prayed instead of just read. Praying God's own words back to Him, incorporating the character of God as I prayed for others. While meditating on God as my Shepherd, I pray that He shepherds those I am praying for. As Healer, I pray for healing over them; it may be physical, mental, financial or spiritual. Worshipping Him as LORD, I pray that He is LORD of my life and theirs. I don't start my day or end it without talking with my Father, Savior, Husband, Lord. Isn't that the way it should be when we love someone?

This guide is meant to be flexible. Pray through the whole thing or divide it up: some sections at night and others in the morning. Or focus on a section you specifically want to target. Make it what you need it to be.

Let the Holy Spirit guide you as you pray. Sometimes He will guide you into a time when it is just about worship and thanksgiving. Other times He will lead you into confession and repentance. There are times when you may have something or someone very specific that you need to spend time in prayer about. Follow where the Spirit leads.

My hope is that your prayers will become richer. Your prayer life more meaningful. We experience God's Presence when we pray. It is essential to everything we do as a Christian.

So let me share with you what this Prayer Devotional is all about and how you can use it and make it your own.

There are 31 separate pages: one for each day of the month. Each day is set up with a different name of God as the theme allowing you to pray with intention through several focus areas; Meditation, Worship, Adoration, and Introspection.

Meditation verses are about recognizing and meditating on who God is and who Jesus is. They come first because it is important to put God first, not just in our prayer life but in everything we do. Meditating on these verses isn't about chanting them over and over again. It's about reading them slowly and deliberately, thinking about what they mean to you and turning them into a prayer. For example: Day 1 Psalm 23:1 "The Lord is my Shepherd." Think about all the ways that God has shepherded you. If nothing comes to mind, you may need to ask God to show you the ways He has been your shepherd. Then turn that into a prayer of praise, thanksgiving and worship.

RECOGNIZING GOD. There are times when I kneel to pray that I am filled with anxiety about many things. Starting with Who God is helps me to pray with perspective. Many names have been attributed to God for this reason – no matter what we are going through, He is capable of meeting us right where we need Him most. When we need comfort, He is our Comforter. When we need healing, He is our Healer. When we feel abandoned, He is our Father. When we feel unlovable, He is Love! Something inside of me changes when I start to pray and I see that that day's name for God is exactly what I needed.

RECOGNIZING JESUS. When we come to see God for all He is, we see Jesus for all He is, too. In John 10:30, Jesus says that He and His Father are one. With these verses lined up side by side, I am able to see how clearly that Jesus and His Father share the same heart. God, the Healer – Jesus heals. The Lord, our Shepherd – Jesus shepherds His sheep. The Lord, our Provider – Jesus, the Bread of Life.

It is easy to pray through these verses quickly. How eager I am to get to the part where I tell God what I want or need. Instead, focus on these verses and let them sink in. This is my God and my Savior. I don't want to miss that. I find that when I give God His due respect, the rest of my prayer is more humble; more willing to be given into His care.

ADORATION and THANKSGIVING. The verses under Worship are divided into verses of adoration and verses of thanksgiving. Adoration is about God's worthiness. Thanksgiving is about what God gives to us or what He does for us. In addition to praying the verses and making them your own, you'll notice that there is a prompt to thank God for things that are personal to you. In the back of this book is a Thanksgiving Log that you can create for yourself. Even if I'm having a bad day, when I start thanking God for the things He has given me and provided for me, it changes my perspective. Giving thanks grounds me. It reminds me that God is good. This is another opportunity to spend time with God. Sometimes when I am praying, I stop right here and use my prayer time to focus on praise and thanksgiving. It becomes a time of pure worship. I save the rest of my devotion for another time.

The last category is Introspection. Once we recognize our heavenly Father for Who He is and what He does for us, then we need to start looking inward at ourselves. These verses aren't easy. You may not like them.

RECOGNIZE MYSELF. The verses under Recognizing Myself get right to the center of our hearts. Hopefully, they reflect who we were before we knew Christ as our Savior but if you recognize yourself now in your present state – it's time to take a serious look inward and ask some serious questions. Don't give in to the temptation to skip through these verses quickly because they make you feel uncomfortable or you don't think they apply to you. Spend a quiet moment here meditating on these verses and inspecting your heart. If you sense conviction; ask yourself why. Let God speak to you. Listen for His voice.

CONFESSION. And then confess. Along with a verse about confession, there is another prompt here to personalize your confession. So often, I've glossed over my actions with a blanket "forgive all my sins" without really facing up to them or recognizing the impact they had on others. But when sins are personalized, it shows that we take them seriously. Naming my sins led me to true repentance. It freed me from something inside me that I didn't even know was there. In some cases, you may need to make amends to someone you've hurt. There's no glossing over it – it's hard and intimidating. But it's a part of our Christian walk. If you have hurt someone in your past and you don't know how to reach them, ask God to bless them over and above the harm you've caused.

Once you've confessed and made amends where possible, you are forgiven and those sins are in your past. If Satan dredges them up and dangles them in front of you [especially when you are trying to sleep] remind him that that was in your past and you don't live there anymore.

HOW GOD SEES ME. The next part of introspection is recognizing how God sees us. This is where I breathe again. After coming through confession, sometimes I wonder how God can stand me. But He does more than that. He looks upon me with love and compassion no matter who I am or how far I've fallen. His Son died in my place. Because of that act of love, my sins are forgiven. He has plans and promises, not just for me but for you; for all of us.

Sometimes this part brings tears to my eyes. I may go back to thanking and praising Him all over again.

Once our hearts are right with God; once we ask for and accept His forgiveness, He can use us. And that leads to My Call.

MY CALL. These verses are about what God has called us to do. As you pray through these verses and make them your own, focus on what you need to follow through with God's call in your life. You are prompted with the question, "What do I need to ask of God to carry this out in my life?"

This is important because, as the saying goes, "God doesn't call the equipped, He equips the called." Let God speak to you during this prayer moment. He will use these verses to prompt you to action. Sometimes the action is to go and do something. Other times, many times in fact, we are called to work on our character; the fruit of the Spirit.[4] The action takes place on the inside. Not everyone is called to be a pastor or missionary, but everyone is called to be patient, kind, loving and forgiving. We are called to live moral lives that honor the Lord. Think carefully on what God has called you to do. Ask Him to equip you. Watch for open doors and opportunities and they will come. Most importantly, be willing.

PROMISE. The next prayer verse is about God's promises. God does not call us and then abandon us. His call to us is followed by promises to help us, to be with us and to never let us go. His promises are a way of equipping us for what He is calling us to do. I find strength and hope in His promises. And remember this; God always keeps His word.

POURING OUT. Emptying our hearts of everything that breaks us, makes us weep and keeps us awake at night. It is last because God must be first; first in our lives and first in our prayer lives. Once we've given God His proper place, once our hearts are right with Him then we can come to Him for anything.[5] It is last because God must be first; first in our lives and first in our prayer lives. Once we've given God His proper place, once our hearts are right with Him then we can ask Him for anything.

---

[4] Galatians 5:22-23 [This is just one passage about the fruit of the Spirit. There are others.

[5] Psalm 66:18, Isaiah 59:2

Personalize the verses in Pouring Out and use them as you pray for those on your prayer list. We pour our hearts out to God for those we love.

Sometimes, I don't always know the immediate need of someone I am praying for. I just know I need to pray for them. On Day One the Pouring Out verse is Psalm 23:4 "Even though I walk through the darkest valley, I will fear no evil, for you are with me; your rod and your staff they comfort me."

I might personalize my prayer something like this, "Lord, I pray for "my friend." I don't know what dark valleys she may be going through right now but I know that you are with her. Be the rod and staff in her hand. Be her comfort. Remove any fears she might have."

Our Lord hears our simple, heartfelt prayers. He answers them according to His will.

And that leads to the most common question asked about prayer; "Why do some prayers go unanswered?" Volumes have been written and preached on this topic so I am only going to briefly add what I have learned.

Sometimes we pray with wrong motives, selfish desires or unconfessed sin. Sometimes it's just not God's will. Sometimes the answer was given and we just don't want to accept it. Sometimes the answer is in the future. A friend of mine shared this prayer with me when she couldn't see God's answer right away, "Lord, thank You for the work I cannot see." Let me repeat that. "Lord, thank you for the work I cannot see." This is probably the most common reason we don't see prayers answered the way we want them to be; God isn't finished!

Please don't mistake my briefness in these explanations of unanswered prayer for being smug or simplifying a complex issue. There are other books that go into depth on this subject. This book is about developing a deeper, richer prayer life that will lead to a deeper relationship with our God and Savior - and answered prayers. Some answers we must wait for. Some requests we just have to let go - trusting in the God who knows us best. And some answers we just can't see.

"Lord, thank You for the work
I cannot see."

The next pages are your thirty-one day prayer devotional followed by directions and the tools for creating your prayer list, an answered prayer log and a thanksgiving list. I recommend you go to these pages next and familiarize yourself with these tools. Start by filling out your prayer list then turn to the current day of the month and begin praying.

I want to encourage you to pray and not give up. Your Heavenly Father hears you and sees you.

DAY 1

Meditation

Recognize God: *Shepherd* Psalm 23:1 The Lord is my Shepherd, I lack nothing.

Recognize Jesus: *The Good Shepherd* John 10:14-15 I am the good shepherd; I know my sheep and my sheep know me – just as the Father knows me and I know the Father – and I lay down my life for the sheep.

Worship

Adoration: Psalm 95:6-7a Come, let us bow down in worship, let us kneel before the LORD our Maker; for he is our God and we are the people of his pasture, the flock under his care.

Give Thanks: Isaiah 40:11 He tends His flock like a shepherd: He gathers the lambs in His arms and carries them close to His heart; He gently leads those that have young.

"What and who am I thankful for? Thank God for them now."

Introspection

Recognize Myself: Psalm 119:176a I have strayed like a lost sheep.

Confession: I Peter 2:24-25 He himself bore our sins in His body on the cross, so that we might die to sins and live for righteousness; by His wounds you have been healed. For you were like sheep going astray, but now you have returned to the Shepherd and Overseer of your souls.

"Confess my sins here. Be specific."

How God Sees Me: Matthew 9:36 When He saw the crowds, He had compassion on them, because they were harassed and helpless, like sheep without a shepherd.

My Call: Titus 3:1-2 Remind the people to be subject to rulers and authorities, to be obedient, to be ready to do whatever is good, to slander no one, to be peaceable and considerate, and always to be gentle toward everyone.

"What do I need to ask of God to carry this out in my life?"

Promise: John 10:27-28 My sheep listen to my voice; I know them, and they follow me. I give them eternal life, and they shall never perish; no one will snatch them out of my hand.

*"What does this promise mean to me?
Be still and listen for God's voice."*

Pouring Out: Psalm 23:4 Even though I walk through the darkest valley, I will fear no evil, for you are with me; your rod and your staff, they comfort me.

DAY 2

Meditation

Recognize God: *Lord of Lords* Deuteronomy 10:17 For the LORD your God is God of gods and Lord of lords, the great God, mighty and awesome, who shows no partiality and accepts no bribes.

Recognize Jesus: *Lord of Lords* Revelation 19:16 On his robe and on his thigh he has this name written: KING OF KINGS AND LORD OF LORDS.

Worship

Adoration: Psalm 99:2-3 Great is the LORD in Zion; He is exalted over all the nations. Let them praise your great and awesome name – He is holy.

Give Thanks: Ephesians 2:8-9 For it is by grace you have been saved, through faith – and this is not from yourselves, it is the gift of God – not by works, so that no one can boast.

"What and who am I thankful for? Thank God for them now."

Introspection

Recognize Myself: Romans 3:23 For all have sinned and fall short of the glory of God.

Confession: Ezekiel 18:27-28 But if a wicked person turns away from the wickedness they have committed and does what is just and right, they will save their life. Because they consider all the offenses they have committed and turn away from them, that person will surely live; they will not die.

"Confess my sins here. Be specific."

How God Sees Me: Ephesians 2:10 For we are God's handiwork, created in Christ Jesus to do good works, which God prepared in advance for us to do.

My Call: I Timothy 4:12 Don't let anyone look down on you because you are young, but set an example for the believers in speech, in conduct, in love, in faith and in purity.

"What do I need to ask of God to carry this out in my life?"

Promise: John 16:22 So with you: Now is your time of grief, but I will see you again and you will rejoice, and no one will take away your joy.

*"What does this promise mean to me?
Be still and listen for God's voice."*

Pouring Out: Psalm 86:2-3 Guard my life, for I am faithful to you; save your servant who trusts in you. You are my God; have mercy on me, Lord, for I call to you all day long.

DAY 3

Meditation

Recognize God: *Lord God Almighty* Amos 4:13 He who forms the mountains, who creates the wind, and who reveals his thoughts to mankind, who turns dawn to darkness, and treads on the heights of the earth – the LORD God Almighty is his name.

Recognize Jesus: *Almighty* Revelation 1:8 "I am the Alpha and the Omega," says the Lord God, "who is and who was and who is to come, the Almighty."

Worship

Adoration: Isaiah 6:3 And they were calling to one another: "Holy, holy, holy is the LORD Almighty; the whole earth is full of his glory."

Give Thanks: Jeremiah 15:16 When your words came, I ate them; they were my joy and my heart's delight, for I bear your name, Lord God Almighty.

"What and who am I thankful for? Thank God for them now."

Introspection

Recognize Myself: Isaiah 6:5 "Woe to me!" I cried. "I am ruined! For I am a man of unclean lips, and I live among a people of unclean lips, and my eyes have seen the King, the LORD Almighty."

Confession: Psalm 80:19 Restore us, Lord God Almighty; make your face shine on us, that we may be saved.

"Confess my sins here. Be specific."

How God Sees Me: II Corinthians 6:18 And, "I will be a Father to you, and you will be my sons and daughters," says the Lord Almighty."

My Call: Amos 5:14 Seek good, not evil, that you may live. Then the LORD God Almighty will be with you, just as you say he is.

"What do I need to ask of God to carry this out in my life?"

Promise: Psalm 84:12 LORD Almighty, blessed is the one who trusts in you.

"What does this promise mean to me? Be still and listen for God's voice."

Pouring Out: Psalm 84:8 Hear my prayer, LORD God Almighty; listen to me, God of Jacob.

DAY 4

Meditation

Recognize God: *Alpha and Omega* Revelation 21:6 He said to me: "It is done. I am the Alpha and the Omega, the Beginning and the End. To the thirsty I will give water without cost from the spring of the water of life."

Recognize Jesus: *Alpha and Omega* Revelation 22:12-13 "Look, I am coming soon! My reward is with me, and I will give to each person according to what they have done. I am the Alpha and the Omega, the First and the Last, the Beginning and the End."

Worship

Adoration: Revelation 4:8b "Holy, holy, holy is the Lord God Almighty, who was, and is, and is to come."

Give Thanks: Revelation 11:17 "We give thanks to you, Lord God Almighty, the One who is and who was, because you have taken your great power and have begun to reign."

"What and who am I thankful for? Thank God for them now."

Introspection

Recognize Myself: Ephesians 5:3 But among you there must not be even a hint of sexual immorality, or of any kind of impurity, or of greed, because these are improper for God's holy people.

Confession: Luke 18:13 But the tax collector stood at a distance. He would not even look up to heaven, but beat his breast and said, "God have mercy on me, a sinner."

"Confess my sins here. Be specific."

How God Sees Me: Luke 15:10 In the same way, I tell you, there is rejoicing in the presence of the angels of God over one sinner who repents."

My Call: Romans 12:2 Do not conform to the pattern of this world but be transformed by the renewing of your mind. Then you will be able to test and approve what God's will is – His good, pleasing and perfect will.

"What do I need to ask of God to carry this out in my life?"

Promise: Philippians 1:6 Being confident of this, that He who began a good work in you will carry it on to completion until the day of Christ Jesus.

*"What does this promise mean to me?
Be still and listen for God's voice."*

Pouring Out: Psalm 25:4-5 Show me your ways, LORD, teach me your paths. Guide me in your truth and teach me, for you are God my Savior, and my hope is in you all day long.

DAY 5

Meditation

Recognize God: *Husband* Isaiah 54:5 For your Maker is your husband – the LORD Almighty is his name – the Holy One of Israel is your Redeemer; he is called God of all the earth.

Recognize Jesus: *Husband* II Corinthians 11:2 I am jealous for you with a godly jealousy. I promised you to one husband, to Christ, so that I might present you as a pure virgin to him.

Worship

Adoration: Psalm 57:9-11 I will praise you, Lord, among the nations; I will sing of you among the peoples. For great is your love, reaching to the heavens; your faithfulness reaches to the skies. Be exalted, O God, above the heavens; let your glory be over all the earth.

Give Thanks: Isaiah 58:11 The LORD will guide you always; He will satisfy your needs in a sun-scorched land and will strengthen your frame. You will be like a well-watered garden, like a spring whose waters never fail.

"What and who am I thankful for? Thank God for them now."

Introspection

Recognize Myself: Jeremiah 2:32 Does a young woman forget her jewelry, a bride her wedding ornaments? Yet my people have forgotten me, days without number.

Confession: Jeremiah 3:14a "Return, faithless people," declares the LORD, "for I am your husband. I will choose you."

"Confess my sins here. Be specific."

How God Sees Me: Isaiah 62:5 As a young man marries a young woman, so will your Builder marry you; as a bridegroom rejoices over his bride, so will your God rejoice over you.

My Call: Romans 12:1 Therefore, I urge you, brothers and sisters, in view of God's mercy, to offer your bodies as a living sacrifice, holy and pleasing to God – this is your true and proper worship.

"What do I need to ask of God to carry this out in my life?"

Promise: Isaiah 41:10 So do not fear, for I am with you; do not be dismayed, for I am your God. I will strengthen you and help you; I will uphold you with my righteous right hand.

*"What does this promise mean to me?
Be still and listen for God's voice."*

Pouring Out: Psalm 17:6 I call on you, my God, for you will answer me; turn your ear to me and hear my prayer.

DAY 6

Meditation

Recognize God: *Creator* Isaiah 40:28 Do you not know? Have you not heard? The LORD is the everlasting God, the Creator of the ends of the earth. He will not grow tired or weary, and His understanding no one can fathom.

Recognize Jesus: *Creator* Colossians 1:16 For in Him all things were created: things in heaven and on earth, visible and invisible, whether thrones or powers or rulers or authorities; all things have been created through Him and for Him.

Worship

Adoration: Psalm 136:4-5 To Him who alone does great wonders, His love endures forever. Who by His understanding made the heavens, His love endures forever.

Thankfulness: Deuteronomy 8:10 When you have eaten and are satisfied, praise the Lord your God for the good land He has given you.

"What and who am I thankful for? Thank God for them now."

Introspection

Recognize Myself: Jeremiah 7:24 But they did not listen or pay attention; instead, they followed the stubborn inclinations of their evil hearts. They went backward and not forward.

Confession: Hebrews 4:13 Nothing in all creation is hidden from God's sight. Everything is uncovered and laid bare before the eyes of Him to whom we must give account.

"Confess my sins here. Be specific."

How God Sees Me: II Corinthians 5:17 Therefore, if anyone is in Christ, the new creation has come. The old has gone, the new is here!

My Call: Ephesians 4:22-23 You were taught, with regard to your former way of life, to put off your old self, which is being corrupted by its deceitful desires; to be made new in the attitude of your minds.

"What do I need to ask of God to carry this out in my life?"

Promise: Jeremiah 29:11 "For I know the plans I have for you," declares the LORD, "plans to prosper you and not to harm you, plans to give you hope and a future."

*"What does this promise mean to me?
Be still and listen for God's voice."*

Pouring Out: Psalm 102:1-2 Hear my prayer, LORD; let my cry for help come to you. Do not hide your face from me when I am in distress. Turn your ear to me; when I call, answer me quickly.

DAY 7

Meditation

Recognize God: God of Peace I Thessalonians 5:23 May God Himself, the God of peace, sanctify you through and through. May your whole spirit, soul and body be kept blameless at the coming of our Lord Jesus Christ.

Recognize Jesus: Peace Ephesians 2:13-14a But now in Christ Jesus you who once were far away have been brought near by the blood of Christ. For He himself is our peace.

Worship

Adoration: Luke 19:38 "Blessed is the king who comes in the name of the Lord! Peace in heaven and glory in the highest!"

Give Thanks: Psalm 4:8 In peace I will lie down and sleep, for you alone, LORD, make me dwell in safety.

"What and who am I thankful for? Thank God for them now."

Introspection

Recognize Myself: Job 3:26 I have no peace, no quietness; I have no rest, but only turmoil.

Confession: Psalm 139:23-24 Search me, O God, and know my heart; test me and know my anxious thoughts. See if there is any offensive way in me, and lead me in the way everlasting.

"Confess my sins here. Be specific."

How God Sees Me: John 14:27 Peace I leave with you; my peace I give you. I do not give to you as the world gives. Do not let your hearts be troubled and do not be afraid.

My Call: Ephesians 6:13-18 Put on the full armor of God – Stand firm with the belt of truth, the breastplate of righteousness, feet fitted with readiness and the gospel of peace. The shield of faith, the helmet of salvation and the sword of the Spirit – the Word of God. Pray in the Spirit! Pray for the saints.

"What do I need to ask of God to carry this out in my life?"

Promise: John 16:33 I have told you these things, so that you may have peace. In this world you will have trouble. But take heart! I have overcome the world.

*"What does this promise mean to me?
Be still and listen for God's voice."*.

Pouring Out: Numbers 6:24-26 "The LORD bless you and keep you; the LORD make his face shine on you and be gracious to you; the LORD turn his face toward you and give you peace."

DAY 8

Meditation

Recognize God: *Living God* Jeremiah 10:10a But the LORD is the true God; He is the living God, the eternal King.

Recognize Jesus: *Son of the Living God* Matthew 16:15-16 "But what about you?" He asked. "Who do you say I am?" Simon Peter answered, "You are the Messiah, the Son of the living God."

Worship

Adoration: Daniel 6:26b "For He is the living God and He endures forever; His kingdom will not be destroyed, His dominion will never end.

Give Thanks: I Peter 1:3 Praise be to the God of our Lord Jesus Christ! In His great mercy He has given us new birth into a living hope through the resurrection of Jesus Christ from the dead.

"What and who am I thankful for? Thank God for them now."

Introspection

Recognize Myself: Mark 7:21-22 For it is from within, out of a person's heart, that evil thoughts come – sexual immorality, theft, murder, adultery, greed, malice, deceit, lewdness, envy, slander, arrogance and folly.

Confession: Hebrews 3:12 See to it, brothers and sisters, that none of you has a sinful, unbelieving heart that turns away from the living God.

> *"Confess my sins here. Be specific."*

How God Sees Me: Romans 9:26 "In the very place where it was said to them, 'You are not my people,' there they will be called 'children of the living God.'"

My Call: Romans 6:13 Do not offer any part of yourself to sin as an instrument of wickedness, but rather offer yourselves to God as those who have been brought from death to life; and offer every part of yourself to Him as an instrument of righteousness.

> *"What do I need to ask of God to carry this out in my life?"*

Promise: Ephesians 2:21-22 In Him the whole body is joined together and rises to become a holy temple in the Lord. And in Him you too are being built together to become a dwelling in which God lives by His Spirit.

> *"What does this promise mean to me?*
> *Be still and listen for God's voice."*

Pouring Out: Psalm 42:2 My soul thirsts for God, for the living God. When can I go and meet with God?

DAY 9

Meditation

Recognize God: *Foundation* Isaiah 33:5-6 The LORD is exalted, for He dwells on high; He will fill Zion with His justice and righteousness. He will be the sure foundation for your times, a rich store of salvation and wisdom and knowledge; the fear of the LORD is the key to this treasure.

Recognize Jesus: *Foundation* I Corinthians 3:11 For no one can lay any foundation other than the one already laid, which is Jesus Christ.

Worship

Adoration: Psalm 89:14 Righteousness and justice are the foundation of your throne; love and faithfulness go before you.

Give Thanks: Ephesians 2:19-20 Consequently, you are no longer foreigners and strangers, but fellow citizens with God's people and also members of His household, built on the foundation of the apostles and prophets, with Christ Jesus Himself as the chief cornerstone.

"What and who am I thankful for? Thank God for them now."

Introspection

Recognize Myself: I Corinthians 10:12-13b So, if you think you are standing firm, be careful that you don't fall! No temptation has overtaken you except what is common to mankind. And God is faithful; He will not let you be tempted beyond what you can bear.

Confession: I John 1:9 If we confess our sins, He is faithful and just to forgive us our sins and to cleanse us from all unrighteousness.

"Confess my sins here. Be specific."

How God Sees Me: Matthew 7:25 The rain came down, the streams rose, and the winds blew and beat against that house; yet it did not fall, because it had its foundation on the rock.

My Call: I Corinthians 16:13 Be on your guard; stand firm in the faith; be courageous; be strong.

"What do I need to ask of God to carry this out in my life?"

Promise: Psalm 37:23 The LORD makes firm the steps of the one who delights in him.

*"What does this promise mean to me?
Be still and listen for God's voice."*

Pouring Out: Psalm 90:17 May the favor of the Lord our God rest on us; establish the work of our hands for us – yes, establish the work of our hands.

DAY 10

Meditation

Recognize God: *Spring of Living Water* Jeremiah 2:13 My people have committed two sins: They have forsaken me, the spring of living water, and have dug their own cisterns, broken cisterns that cannot hold water.

Recognize Jesus: *Living Water* John 7:38 "Whoever believes in me, as Scripture has said, rivers of living water will flow from within them."

Worship

Adoration: Psalm 63:1 You, God, are my God, earnestly I seek you; I thirst for you, my whole being longs for you, in a dry and parched land where there is no water.

Give Thanks: Psalm 107:8-9 Let them give thanks to the LORD for his unfailing love and his wonderful deeds for mankind, for he satisfies the thirsty and fills the hungry with good things.

"What and who am I thankful for? Thank God for them now."

Introspection

Recognize Myself: Psalm 107:5 They were hungry and thirsty, and their lives ebbed away.

Confession: James 4:8 Come near to God and He will come near to you. Wash your hands, you sinners, and purify your hearts, you double-minded.

"Confess my sins here. Be specific."

How God Sees Me: John 4:14 But whoever drinks the water I give them will never thirst. Indeed, the water I give them will become in them a spring of water welling up to eternal life.

My Call: Proverbs 25:21 If your enemy is hungry, give him food to eat; if he is thirsty, give him water to drink.

"What do I need to ask of God to carry this out in my life?"

Promise: Revelation 7:17 For the Lamb at the center of the throne will be their shepherd; He will lead them to springs of living water. And God will wipe away every tear from their eyes.

"What does this promise mean to me? Be still and listen for God's voice."

Pouring Out: Psalm 42:1-2 As the deer pants for streams of water, so my soul pants for you, my God. My soul thirsts for God, for the living God. When can I go and meet with God?

DAY 11

Meditation

Recognize God: *God Over All* Isaiah 37:16 "LORD Almighty, the God of Israel… you alone are God over all the kingdoms of the earth. You have made heaven and earth.

Recognize Jesus: *God Over All* Romans 9:5 Theirs are the patriarchs, and from them is traced the human ancestry of the Messiah, who is God over all, forever praised! Amen.

Worship

Adoration: I Chronicles 29:11 Yours, LORD, is the greatness and the power and the glory and the majesty and the splendor, for everything in heaven and earth is yours. Yours, LORD, is the kingdom; you are exalted as head over all.

Give Thanks: Romans 8:28 And we know that in all things God works for the good of those who love Him, who have been called according to His purpose.

"What and who am I thankful for? Thank God for them now."

Introspection

Recognize Myself: Ephesians 2:1-2 As for you, you were dead in your transgressions and sins in which you used to live when you followed the ways of this world and the ruler of the kingdom of the air, the spirit who is now at work in those who are disobedient.

Confession: Psalm 32:5 Then I acknowledged my sin to you and did not cover up my iniquity. I said, "I will confess my transgressions to the LORD." And you forgave the guilt of my sin.

"Confess my sins here. Be specific."

How God Sees Us: Ephesians 1:4 For He chose us in Him before the creation of the world to be holy and blameless in his sight.

My Call: I Peter 2:11-12 Dear friends, I urge you… to abstain from sinful desires, which wage war against your soul. Live such good lives among the pagans that, though they accuse you of doing wrong, they may see your good deeds and glorify God on the day he visits us.

"What do I need to ask of God to carry this out in my life?"

Promise: II Corinthians 9:8 And God is able to bless you abundantly, so that in all things at all times, having all that you need, you will abound in every good work.

*"What does this promise mean to me?
Be still and listen for God's voice."*

Pouring Out: Psalm 145:18-19 The LORD is near to all who call on Him, to all who call on Him in truth. He fulfills the desires of those who fear Him; He hears their cry and saves them.

DAY 12

Meditation

Recognize God: *LORD* Psalm 83:18 Let them know that you, whose name is the LORD – that you alone are the Most High over all the earth.

Recognize Jesus: *Lord* Philippians 2:10-11 That at the name of Jesus every knee should bow, in heaven and on earth and under the earth, and every tongue acknowledge that Jesus Christ is Lord, to the glory of God the Father.

Worship

Adoration: Psalm 150:1-2,6 Praise the LORD. Praise God in His sanctuary; praise Him in His mighty heavens. Praise Him for His acts of power; praise Him for his surpassing greatness…Let everything that has breath praise the LORD. Praise the LORD.

Give Thanks: Psalm 107:1 Give thanks to the LORD, for He is good; His love endures forever.

"What and who am I thankful for? Thank God for them now."

Introspection

Recognize Myself: Exodus 20:7 "You shall not misuse the name of the LORD your God, for the LORD will not hold anyone guiltless who misuses his name.

Confession: Daniel 9:19 Lord, listen! Lord, forgive! Lord, hear and act! For your sake, my God, do not delay, because your city and your people bear your Name.

"Confess my sins here. Be specific."

How God Sees Me: Isaiah 43:1-2 But now, this is what the Lord says – "Do not fear, for I have redeemed you; I have summoned you by name; you are mine.

My Call: Acts 2:38-39 "Repent and be baptized, every one of you, in the name of Jesus Christ for the forgiveness of your sins. And you will receive the gift of the Holy Spirit. The promise is for you and your children and for all who are far off – for all whom the Lord will call.

"What do I need to ask of God to carry this out in my life?"

Promise: Deuteronomy 4:29 But if from there you seek the LORD your God, you will find Him if you seek Him with all your heart and with all your soul.

*"What does this promise mean to me?
Be still and listen for God's voice."*

Pouring Out: I Kings 8:28 Yet give attention to your servant's prayer and his plea for mercy, LORD my God. Hear the cry and the prayer that your servant is praying in your presence this day.

DAY 13

Meditation

Recognize God: *Holy One* Isaiah 48:17 This is what the LORD says – your Redeemer, the Holy One of Israel: "I am the LORD your God, who teaches you what is best for you, who directs you in the way you should go."

Recognize Jesus: *Holy One* John 6:68-69 Simon Peter answered Him, "Lord, to whom shall we go? You have the words of eternal life. We have come to believe and to know that you are the Holy One of God.

Worship

Adoration: Isaiah 12:6 Shout aloud and sing for joy, people of Zion, for great is the Holy One of Israel among you.

Thankfulness: II Corinthians 9:11 You will be enriched in every way so that you can be generous on every occasion, and through us your generosity will result in thanksgiving to God.

"What and who am I thankful for? Thank God for them now."

Introspection

Recognize Myself: Psalm 78:40-41 How often they rebelled against Him in the wilderness and grieved Him in the wasteland! Again and again they put God to the test; they vexed the Holy One of Israel.

Confession: Ezekiel 14:6 This is what the sovereign LORD says: Repent! Turn from your idols and renounce all your detestable practices!

"Confess my sins here. Be specific."

How God Sees Me: Ephesians 2:4-5 But because of His great love for us, God, who is rich in mercy, made us alive with Christ even when we were dead in transgressions – it is by grace you have been saved.

My Call: I Thessalonians 4:7 For God did not call us to be impure, but to live a holy life.

"What do I need to ask of God to carry this out in my life?"

Promise: Job 8:7 Your beginnings will seem humble, so prosperous will your future be.

*"What does this promise mean to me?
Be still and listen for God's voice."*

Pouring Out: I Samuel 12:23 As for me, far be it from me that I should sin against the LORD by failing to pray for you. And I will teach you the way that is good and right.

DAY 14

Meditation

Recognize God: *Judge* Isaiah 33:22 For the LORD is our judge, the LORD is our lawgiver, the LORD is our king; it is He who will save us.

Recognize Jesus: *Judge* Acts 10:40, 42 But God raised Him from the dead on the third day and caused him to be seen… He commanded us to preach to the people and to testify that He is the one who God appointed as judge of the living and the dead.
Worship

Adoration: Psalm 96:10 Say among the nations, "The LORD reigns." The world is firmly established, it cannot be moved; He will judge the peoples with equity.

Thankfulness: Psalm 68:19-20 Praise be to the Lord, to God our Savior, who daily bears our burdens. Our God is a God who saves; from the Sovereign LORD comes escape from death.

"What and who am I thankful for? Thank God for them now."

Introspection

Recognize Myself: II Corinthians 5:10 For we all must appear before the judgment seat of Christ, so that each of us may receive what is due us for the things done while in the body, whether good or bad.

Confession: Psalm 51:3-4 For I know my transgressions, and my sin is always before me. Against You, You only have I sinned and done what is evil in your sight; so you are right in your verdict and justified when you judge.

"Confess my sins here. Be specific."

How God Sees Me: Isaiah 43:4 Since you are precious and honored in my sight, and because I love you, I will give people in exchange for you, nations in exchange for your life.

My Call: Matthew 6:14 For if you forgive other people when they sin against you, your heavenly Father will also forgive you.

"What do I need to ask of God to carry this out in my life?"

Promise: II Timothy 4:8 Now there is in store for me the crown of righteousness, which the Lord, the righteous Judge, will award to me on that day – and not only to me, but also to all who have longed for his appearing.

*"What does this promise mean to me?
Be still and listen for God's voice."*

Pouring Out: Psalm 116:1-2 I love the LORD, for He heard my voice; he heard my cry for mercy. Because He turned His ear to me, I will call on Him as long as I live.

DAY 15

Meditation

Recognize God: *I AM* Exodus 3:14 God said to Moses, "I AM who I AM. This is what you are to say to the Israelites: 'I AM has sent me to you."

Recognize Jesus: *I AM* Mark 14:61b-62a "Are you the Christ? The Son of the Blessed One?" "I am," said Jesus.

Worship

Adoration: Psalm 29:2 Ascribe to the LORD the glory due His name; worship the LORD in the splendor of His holiness.

Give Thanks: I Chronicles 29:14 "But who am I, and who are my people, that we should be able to give as generously as this? Everything comes from you, and we have given you only what comes from your hand."

"What and who am I thankful for? Thank God for them now."

Introspection

Recognize Myself: Titus 3:3 At one time we too were foolish, disobedient, deceived and enslaved by all kinds of passions and pleasures. We lived in malice and envy, being hated and hating one another.

Confession: Psalm 31:9 Be merciful to me, LORD, for I am in distress; my eyes grow weak with sorrow, my soul and body with grief.

"Confess my sins here. Be specific."

How God Sees Me: Daniel 9:9 The Lord our God is merciful and forgiving, even though we have rebelled against him.

My Call: I Peter 4:10 Each of you should use whatever gift you have received to serve others, as faithful stewards of God's grace in its various forms.

"What do I need to ask of God to carry this out in my life?"

Promise: Jeremiah 1:19 They will fight against you but will not overcome you, for I am with you and will rescue you, declares the LORD.

*"What does this promise mean to me?
Be still and listen for God's voice."*

Pouring Out: II Thessalonians 1:11 With this in mind, we constantly pray for you, that our God may make you worthy of His calling, and that by His power He may bring to fruition your every desire for goodness and your every deed prompted by faith.

DAY 16

Meditation

Recognize God: *King* Psalm 47:7-8 For God is the King of all the earth; sing to Him a psalm of praise. God reigns over the nations; God is seated on His holy throne.

Recognize Jesus: *King* Jeremiah 23:5 "The days are coming," declares the LORD, "when I will raise up for David a righteous Branch, a King who will reign wisely and do what is just and right in the land."

Worship

Adoration: Psalm 95:2-3 Let us come before Him with thanksgiving and extol Him with music and song. For the LORD is the great God, the great King above all gods.

Give Thanks: I Chronicles 29: 12-13 Wealth and honor come from you; you are the ruler of all things. In your hands are strength and power to exalt and give strength to all. Now, our God, we give thanks, and praise your glorious name.

"What and who am I thankful for? Thank God for them now."

Introspection

Recognize Myself: Isaiah 59:2 But your iniquities have separated you from God; your sins have hidden His face from you, so that He will not hear.

Confession: Proverbs 28:13-14 Whoever conceals their sins does not prosper but the one who confesses and renounces them finds mercy. Blessed is the one who always trembles before God, but whoever hardens their heart falls into trouble.

"Confess my sins here. Be specific."

How God Sees Me: Deuteronomy 7:6 For you are a people holy to the LORD your God. The LORD your God has chosen you out of all the peoples on the face of the earth to be His people, His treasured possession.

My Call: Matthew 6:33 But seek first His kingdom and His righteousness, and all these things will be given to you as well.

"What do I need to ask of God to carry this out in my life?"

Promise: Zechariah 9:16 The LORD their God will save His people on that day as a shepherd saves his flock. They will sparkle in His land like jewels in a crown.

*"What does this promise mean to me?
Be still and listen for God's voice."*

Pouring Out: Lamentations 3:54-56 The waters closed over my head, and I thought I was about to perish. I called on your name, Lord, from the depths of the pit. You heard my plea: "Do not close your ears to my cry for relief."

DAY 17

Meditation

Recognize God: *Deliverer* Psalm 144:2 He is my loving God and my fortress, my stronghold and my deliverer, my shield, in whom I take refuge, who subdues peoples under me.

Recognize Jesus: *Messiah (Deliverer)* John 20:31 But these are written that you may believe that Jesus is the Messiah, the Son of God, and that by believing you may have life in His name.

Worship

Adoration: Deuteronomy 32:3 I will proclaim the name of the LORD. Oh, praise the greatness of our God!

Give Thanks: Romans 7:25a Thanks be to God, who delivers me through Jesus Christ our Lord!

"What and who am I thankful for? Thank God for them now."

Introspection

Recognize Myself: Psalm 38:17-18 For I am about to fall, and my pain is ever with me. I confess my iniquity; I am troubled by my sin.

Confession: Psalm 79:9 Help us, God our Savior, for the glory of your name; deliver us and forgive our sins for your name's sake.

"Confess my sins here. Be specific."

How God Sees Me: Psalm 116:8 For you, LORD, have delivered me from death, my eyes from tears, my feet from stumbling.

My Call: Romans 13:13 Let us behave decently, as in daytime, not in carousing and drunkenness, not in sexual immorality and debauchery, not in dissension and jealousy.

"What do I need to ask of God to carry this out in my life?"

Promise: Joel 2:32 And everyone who calls on the name of the LORD will be saved; for on Mount Zion and in Jerusalem there will be deliverance, as the LORD has said, even among the survivors whom the Lord calls.

*"What does this promise mean to me?
Be still and listen for God's voice."*

Pouring Out: Psalm 40:17 But as for me, I am poor and needy; may the Lord think of me. You are my help and my deliverer; you are my God, do not delay.

DAY 18

Meditation

Recognize God: *Lord of all* Romans 10:12 For there is no difference between Jew and Gentile – the same Lord is Lord of all and richly blesses all who call on him.

Recognize Jesus: *Lord of all* Acts 10:36 You know the message God sent to the people of Israel, announcing the good news of peace through Jesus Christ, who is Lord of all.

Worship

Adoration: Revelation 15:3-4 "Great and marvelous are your deeds, LORD God Almighty. Just and true are your ways, King of the nations. Who will not fear you, Lord, and bring glory to your name? For you alone are holy. All nations will come and worship before you, for your righteous acts have been revealed.

Give Thanks: Exodus 15:2 The Lord is my strength and my defense; he has become my salvation. He is my God, and I will praise him, my father's God and I will exalt him.

"For what and who am I thankful for? Thank God for them now."

Introspection

Recognize Myself: Romans 3:10-12 There is no one righteous, not even one; there is no one who understands; there is no one who seeks God. All have turned away, they have together become worthless; there is no one who does good, not even one.

Confession: Ezra 10:1 While Ezra was praying and confessing, weeping and throwing himself down before the house of God, a large crowd of Israelites – men, women and children – gathered around him. They too wept bitterly.

"Confess my sins here. Be specific."

How God Sees Me: John 1:12 Yet to all who did receive him, to those who believed in his name, he gave the right to become children of God.

My Call: Luke 9:23 Then he said to them all: Whoever wants to be my disciple must deny themselves and take up their cross daily and follow me.

"What do I need to ask of God to carry this out in my life?"

Promise: Isaiah 41:33 I am the Lord your God. I am holding your right hand. I tell you, "Don't be afraid, I will help you."

*"What does this promise mean to me?
Be still and listen for God's voice."*

Pouring Out: Psalm 86:11 Teach me your way, LORD, that I may rely on your faithfulness: give me an undivided heart, that I may fear your name.

DAY 19

Meditation

Recognize God: *The Lord our Righteousness* Jeremiah 23:6 In His days Judah will be saved and Israel will live in safety. This is the name by which He will be called: The LORD Our Righteous Savior.

Recognize Jesus: *Righteousness* I Corinthians 1:30 It is because of him that you are in Christ Jesus, who has become for us wisdom from God – that is, our righteousness, holiness and redemption.

Worship

Adoration: Psalm 7:17 I will give thanks to the LORD because of His righteousness; I will sing the praises of the name of the LORD Most High.

Give Thanks: Isaiah 61:11 For as the soil makes the sprout come up and a garden causes seeds to grow, so the Sovereign Lord will make righteousness and praise spring up before all nations.

"What and who am I thankful for? Thank God for them now."

Introspection

Recognize Myself: Proverbs 15:9 The LORD detests the way of the wicked, but He loves those who pursue righteousness.

Confession: Psalm 143:11 For your name's sake, Lord, preserve my life; in your righteousness, bring me out of trouble.

"Confess my sins here. Be specific."

How God Sees Me: Isaiah 42:6 "I, the LORD, have called you in righteousness; I will take hold of your hand. I will keep you and will make you to be a covenant for the people and a light for the Gentiles.

My Call: II Timothy 2:22 Flee the evil desires of youth and pursue righteousness, faith, love and peace, along with those who call on the Lord out of a pure heart.

"What do I need to ask of God to carry this out in my life?"

Promise: Matthew 5:6 Blessed are those who hunger and thirst for righteousness, for they will be filled.

*"What does this promise mean to me?
Be still and listen for God's voice."*

Pouring Out: Psalm 143:1 LORD, hear my prayer, listen to my cry for mercy; in your faithfulness and righteousness come to my relief.

DAY 20

Meditation

Recognize God: *Healer* Exodus 15:26 He said, "If you listen carefully to the LORD your God and do what is right in His eyes, if you pay attention to His commands and keep all His decrees, I will not bring on you any of the diseases I brought on the Egyptians, for I am the LORD, who heals you."

Recognize Jesus: Healer Matthew 9:35 Jesus went through all the towns and villages, teaching in their synagogues, proclaiming the good news of the kingdom, and healing every disease and sickness.

Worship

Adoration: Isaiah 49:13 Shout for joy, you heavens; rejoice, you earth; burst into song, you mountains! For the LORD comforts His people and will have compassion on His afflicted ones.

Give Thanks: Psalm 103:1-3 Praise the Lord, my soul; all my inmost being, praise His holy name. Praise the LORD, my soul, and forget not all His benefits – who forgives all your sins and heals all your diseases.

"What and who am I thankful for? Thank God for them now."

Introspection

Recognize Myself: Job 4:20 Between dawn and dusk they are broken to pieces; unnoticed, they perish forever.

Confession: Romans 7:24 What a wretched man I am! Who will rescue me from this body that is subject to death?

"Confess my sins here. Be specific."

How God Sees Me: Psalm 103:2-4 Praise the Lord, my soul, and forget not all His benefits - who forgives all your sins and heals all your diseases, who redeems your life from the pit and crowns you with love and compassion.

My Call: Isaiah 6:8 Then I heard the voice of the LORD saying, "Whom shall I send? And who will go for us?" And I said, "Here am I. Send me!"

"What do I need to ask of God to carry this out in my life?"

Promise: II Corinthians 12:9 But He said to me, "My grace is sufficient for you, for my power is made perfect in weakness." Therefore I will boast all the more gladly about my weaknesses, so that Christ's power may rest on me.

*"What does this promise mean to me?
Be still and listen for God's voice."*

Pouring Out: Jeremiah 17:14 Heal me, LORD, and I will be healed; save me and I will be saved, for You are the one I praise.

DAY 21

Meditation

Recognize God: *Redeemer* Isaiah 44:24 "This is what the LORD says – your Redeemer, who formed you in the womb: I am the LORD, the Maker of all things, who stretches out the heavens, who spreads out the earth by myself."

Recognize Jesus: *Redeemer* Galatians 3:13 Christ redeemed us from the curse of the law by becoming a curse for us, for it is written: "Cursed is everyone who is hung on a pole."

Worship

Adoration: Exodus 15:11 Who among the gods is like you, LORD? Who is like you – majestic in holiness, awesome in glory, working wonders?

Give Thanks: Exodus 15:13 In your unfailing love you will lead the people You have redeemed. In your strength You will guide them to your holy dwelling.

"What and who am I thankful for? Thank God for them now."

Introspection

Recognize Myself: Isaiah 52:3 For this is what the LORD says: "You were sold for nothing, and without money you will be redeemed."

Confession: Isaiah 44:22 I have swept away your offenses like a cloud, your sins like the morning mist. Return to me, for I have redeemed you.

"Confess my sins here. Be specific."

How God Sees Me: Romans 8:1-2 Therefore, there is now no condemnation for those who are in Christ Jesus, because through Christ Jesus the law of the Spirit who gives life has set you free from the law of sin and death.

My Call: Colossians 3:1-3 Since, then, you have been raised with Christ, set your hearts on things above, where Christ is, seated at the right hand of God. Set your minds on things above, not on earthly things. For you died, and your life is now hidden with Christ in God.

"What do I need to ask of God to carry this out in my life?"

Promise: Job 19:25 I know that my redeemer lives, and that in the end He will stand on the earth.

*"What does this promise mean to me?
Be still and listen for God's voice."*

Pouring Out: Psalm 55:16-17 As for me, I call to God, and the LORD saves me. Evening, morning and noon I cry out in distress, and He hears my voice.

DAY 22

Meditation

Recognize God: *Rock* Deuteronomy 32:4 He is the Rock, His works are perfect, and all His ways are just. A faithful God who does no wrong, upright and just is He.

Recognize Jesus: *Rock* I Corinthians 10:3-4 They all ate the same spiritual food and drank the same spiritual drink; for they drank from the spiritual rock that accompanied them, and that rock was Christ.

Worship

Adoration: I Samuel 2:2 There is no one holy like the LORD; there is no one besides you; there is no Rock like our God.

Give Thanks: Psalm 18:1-2 I love you, LORD, my strength. The LORD is my rock, my fortress and my deliverer; my God is my rock, in whom I take refuge, my shield and the horn of my salvation, my stronghold.

"What and who am I thankful for? Thank God for them now."

Introspection

Recognize Myself: Deuteronomy 32:18 You deserted the Rock, who fathered you; you forgot the God who gave you birth.

Confession: Psalm 19: 12,14 But who can discern their own errors? Forgive my hidden faults. May these words of my mouth and this meditation of my heart be pleasing in your sight, Lord, my Rock and my Redeemer.

"Confess my sins here. Be specific."

How God Sees Me: I Corinthians 3:16 Don't you know that you are God's temple and that God's Spirit dwells in your midst?

My Call: Matthew 28:19-20a Therefore go and make disciples of all nations, baptizing them in the name of the Father and of the Son and of the Holy Spirit, and teaching them to obey everything I have commanded you.

"What do I need to ask of God to carry this out in my life?"

Promise: Matthew 28:20b And surely I am with you always, to the very end of the age.

"What does this promise mean to me? Be still and listen for God's voice."

Pouring Out: Psalm 61:1-3 Hear my cry, O God; listen to my prayer. From the ends of the earth I call to you, I call as my heart grows faint; lead me to the rock that is higher than I. For you have been my refuge, a strong tower against the foe.

DAY 23

Meditation

Recognize God: *Savior* II Samuel 22:3 My God is my rock, in whom I take refuge, my shield and the horn of my salvation. He is my stronghold, my refuge and my savior.

Recognize Jesus: *Savior* Titus 2:13-14 While we wait for the blessed hope – the appearing of the glory of our great God and Savior, Jesus Christ, who gave Himself for us to redeem us from all wickedness and to purify for Himself a people that are His very own, eager to do what is good.

Worship

Adoration: Psalm 18:46 The LORD lives! Praise be to my Rock! Exalted be God my Savior.

Give Thanks: Titus 3:5-6 He saved us, not because of righteous things we had done, but because of His mercy. He saved us through the washing of rebirth and renewal by the Holy Spirit, whom He poured out on us generously through Jesus Christ our Savior.

"What and who am I thankful for? Thank God for them now."

Introspection

Recognize Myself: I Timothy 1:15 Here is a trustworthy saying that deserves full acceptance: Christ Jesus came into the world to save sinners – of whom I am the worst.

Confession: Psalm 4:1 Answer me when I call to you, my righteous God. Give me relief from my distress; have mercy on me and hear my prayer.

"Confess my sins here. Be specific."

How God Sees Me: Titus 3:4-6 But when the kindness and love of God our Savior appeared, He saved us, not because of righteous things we had done, but because of His mercy. He saved us through the washing of rebirth and renewal by the Holy Spirit, whom He poured out on us generously through Jesus Christ our Savior.

My Call: II Peter 3:18 But grow in grace and knowledge of our Lord and Savior Jesus Christ. To Him be glory both now and forevermore! Amen.

"What do I need to ask of God to carry this out in my life?"

Promise: Romans 10:9 If you declare with your mouth, "Jesus is Lord," and believe in your heart that God raised Him from the dead, you will be saved.

*"What does this promise mean to me?
Be still and listen for God's voice."*

Pouring Out: I Chronicles 16:35 Cry out, "Save us, God our Savior; gather us and deliver us from the nations, that we may give thanks to your holy name, and glory in your praise."

DAY 24

Meditation

Recognize God: *Provider* Genesis 22:14 So Abraham called that place The LORD Will Provide. And to this day it is said, "On the mountain of the LORD it will be provided."

Recognize Jesus: *Bread of Life* John 6:35 Then Jesus declared, "I am the bread of life. Whoever comes to me will never go hungry, and whoever believes in me will never be thirsty."

Worship

Adoration: Psalm 68:35 You, God, are awesome in your sanctuary; the God of Israel gives power and strength to his people. Praise be to God!

Give Thanks: Matthew 6:31-32 So do not worry, saying, 'What shall we eat?' or 'What shall we drink?' or 'What shall we wear?' ... Your heavenly Father knows that you need them.

"What and who am I thankful for? Thank God for them now."

Introspection

Recognize Myself: Haggai 1:5-6 Now this is what the LORD Almighty says: "Give careful thought to your ways. You have planted much, but harvested little. You eat, but never have enough. You drink, but never have your fill. You put on clothes, but are not warm. You earn wages, only to put them in a purse with holes in it.

Confession: Psalm 51:10-12 Create in me a pure heart, O God, and renew a steadfast spirit within me. Do not cast me from your presence or take your Holy Spirit from me. Restore to me the joy of your salvation and grant me a willing spirit, to sustain me.

"Confess my sins here. Be specific."

How God Sees Me: Job 10:12 You gave me life and showed me kindness, and in your providence watched over my spirit.

My Call: Mark 1:17-18 "Come, follow me," Jesus said, "and I will send you out to fish for people. At once they left their nets and followed him.

"What do I need to ask of God to carry this out in my life?"

Promise: Philippians 4:19 And my God will meet all your needs according to the riches of his glory in Christ Jesus.

*"What does this promise mean to me?
Be still and listen for God's voice."*

Pouring Out: Philippians 4:6 Do not be anxious about anything, but in every situation, by prayer and petition, with thanksgiving, present your requests to God.

DAY 25

Meditation

Recognize God: *Mighty God* Jeremiah 32:18b -19a Great and mighty God, whose name is the LORD Almighty, great are your purposes and mighty are your deeds.

Recognize Jesus: *Mighty God* Isaiah 9:6 For to us a child is born, to us a son is given, and the government will be on His shoulders. And He will be called Wonderful Counselor, Mighty God, Everlasting Father, Prince of Peace.

Worship

Adoration: Psalm 89:8 Who is like you, LORD God Almighty? You, LORD, are mighty, and your faithfulness surrounds you.

Give Thanks: Ephesians 1:3 Praise be to the God and Father of our Lord Jesus Christ, who has blessed us in the heavenly realms with every spiritual blessing in Christ.

"What and who am I thankful for? Thank God for them now."

Introspection

Recognize Myself: I John 1:8 If we claim to be without sin, we deceive ourselves and the truth is not in us.

Confession: Daniel 9:15 Now, Lord our God, who brought your people out of Egypt with a mighty hand and who made for yourself a name that endures to this day, we have sinned, we have done wrong.

"Confess my sins here. Be specific."

How God Sees Me: John 15:16 You did not choose me, but I chose you and appointed you so that you might go and bear fruit – fruit that will last – and so that whatever you ask in my name the Father will give you.

My Call: John 15: 12 My command is this: Love each other as I have loved you.

"What do I need to ask of God to carry this out in my life?"

Promise: I John 3:2 Dear friends, now we are children of God, and what we will be has not yet been made known. But we know that when Christ appears, we shall be like Him, for we shall see Him as He is.

*"What does this promise mean to me?
Be still and listen for God's voice."*

Pouring Out: Nehemiah 9:32a "Now therefore, our God, the great God, mighty and awesome, who keeps His covenant of love, do not let all this hardship seem trifling in your eyes."

DAY 26

Meditation

Recognize God: *Father* Isaiah 64:8 Yet you, LORD, are our Father. We are the clay, you are the potter; we are all the work of your hand.

Recognize Jesus: *Son* II Peter 1:17 He received honor and glory from God the Father when the voice came to Him from the Majestic Glory, saying, "This is my Son, whom I love; with Him I am well pleased."

Worship

Adoration: Psalm 40:5 Many, LORD my God, are the wonders you have done, the things you planned for us. None can compare with you; were I to speak and tell of your deeds, they would be too many to declare.

Give Thanks: Matthew 6:26 Look at the birds of the air; they do not sow or reap or store away in barns, and yet your heavenly Father feeds them. Are you not much more valuable than they?

"What and who am I thankful for? Thank God for them now."

Introspection

Recognize Myself: Luke 5:22 Jesus knew what they were thinking and asked, "Why are you thinking these things in your hearts?"

Confession: Luke 15:18 I will set out and go back to my father and say to him: Father, I have sinned against heaven and against you.

"Confess my sins here. Be specific."

How God Sees Me: I John 3:1 See what great love the Father has lavished on us, that we should be called children of God! And that is what we are! The reason the world did not know us is that it did not know Him.

My Call: Matthew 5:44-45a But I tell you, love your enemies and pray for those who persecute you, that you may be children of your Father in heaven.

"What do I need to ask of God to carry this out in my life?"

Promise: Psalm 94:14 For the LORD will not reject his people; He will never forsake His inheritance.

*"What does this promise mean to me?
Be still and listen for God's voice."*

Pouring Out: Psalm 25:1-2 In you, LORD my God, I put my trust. I trust in you; do not let me be put to shame, nor let my enemies triumph over me.

DAY 27

Meditation

Recognize God: *Light* I John 1:5 This is the message we have heard from Him and declare to you: God is light; in Him there is no darkness at all.

Recognize Jesus: *Light of the World* John 8:12 When Jesus spoke again to the people, He said, "I am the light of the world. Whoever follows me will never walk in darkness, but will have the light of life.

Worship

Adoration: Revelation 7:12 "Amen! Praise and glory and wisdom and thanks and honor and power and strength be to our God forever and ever. Amen!"

Thankfulness: Matthew 4:16 The people living in darkness have seen a great light; on those living in the land of the shadow of death a light has dawned."

"What and who am I thankful for? Thank God for them now."

Introspection

Recognize Myself: John 3:19 This is the verdict: Light has come into the world, but people loved darkness instead of light because their deeds were evil.

Confession: Psalm 51:7-9 Cleanse me with hyssop, and I will be clean; wash me, and I will be whiter than snow. Let me hear joy and gladness; let the bones you have crushed rejoice. Hide your face from my sins and blot out all my iniquity.

> *"Confess my sins here. Be specific."*

How God Sees Me: Matthew 5:14 You are the light of the world. A town built on a hill cannot be hidden.

My Call: Matthew 5:16 In the same way, let your light shine before others, that they may see your good deeds and glorify your Father in heaven.

> *"What do I need to ask of God to carry this out in my life?"*

Promise: I John 1:7 But if we walk in the light as He is in the light, we have fellowship with one another, and the blood of Jesus Christ His Son cleanses us from all sin.

> "What does this promise mean to me?
> Be still and listen for God's voice."

Pouring Out: Lamentations 5:1 Remember, LORD, what has happened to us; look, and see our disgrace.

DAY 28

Meditation

Recognize God: *The God Most High* Psalm 78:35 They remembered that God was their Rock, that God Most High was their Redeemer.

Recognize Jesus: *Son of the Most High* Luke 1:32 He will be great and will be called the Son of the Most High. The Lord God will give him the throne of his father David.

Worship

Adoration: Psalm 93:1 The LORD reigns, he is robed in majesty; the LORD is robed in majesty and armed with strength; indeed, the world is established, firm and secure.

Give Thanks: Psalm 66:18-20 If I had cherished sin in my heart, the Lord would not have listened; but God has surely listened and has heard my prayer. Praise be to God, who has not rejected my prayer or withheld his love from me!

"What and who am I thankful for? Thank God for them now."

Introspection

Recognize Myself: Matthew 15:19 For out of the heart come evil thoughts – murder, adultery, sexual immorality, theft, false testimony, slander.

Confession: Ezra 9:6 "I am too ashamed and disgraced, my God, to lift up my face to you, because our sins are higher than our heads and our guilt has reached to the heavens.

"Confess my sins here. Be specific."

How God Sees Me: John 3:16 For God so loved the world that He gave his one and only Son, that whoever believes in Him shall not perish but have eternal life.

My Call: Luke 6:35 But love your enemies, do good to them, and lend to them without expecting to get anything back. Then your reward will be great, and you will be children of the Most High, because he is kind to the ungrateful and wicked.

"What do I need to ask of God to carry this out in my life?"

Promise: James 4:10 Humble yourselves before the Lord and he will lift you up.

*"What does this promise mean to me?
Be still and listen for God's voice."*

Pouring Out: Psalm 143:10 Teach me to do your will, for you are my God; may your good Spirit lead me on level ground.

DAY 29

Meditation

Recognize God: *Love* I John 4:16 And so we know and rely on the love God has for us. God is love. Whoever lives in love lives in God, and God in them.

Recognize Jesus: *Love* I John 3:16 This is how we know what love is: Jesus Christ laid down His life for us. And we ought to lay down our lives for our brothers and sisters.

Worship

Adoration: I Chronicles 16:34 Give thanks to the Lord, for He is good; His love endures forever.

Give Thanks: Romans 8:38-39 For I am convinced that neither death nor life, neither angels nor demons, neither the present nor the future, nor any powers, neither height nor depth, nor anything else in all creation, will be able to separate us from the love of God that is in Christ Jesus our Lord.

"What and who am I thankful for? Thank God for them now."

Introspection

Recognize Myself: I Corinthians 13:1 If I speak in the tongues of men and of angels, but do not have love, I am only a resounding gong or a clanging cymbal.

Confession: Psalm 51:1-2 Have mercy on my, O God, according to your unfailing love; according to your great compassion blot out my transgressions. Wash away all my iniquity and cleanse me from my sin.

"Confess my sins here. Be specific."

How God Sees Me: Jeremiah 31:3 The LORD appeared to us in the past, saying: "I have loved you with an everlasting love; I have drawn you with unfailing kindness.

My Call: Mark 12: 30-31 Love the Lord your God with all your heart and with all your soul and with all your mind and with all your strength. The second is this: Love your neighbor as yourself.

"What do I need to ask of God to carry this out in my life?"

Promise: John 8:36 "So if the Son sets you free, you will be free indeed."

*"What does this promise mean to me?
Be still and listen for God's voice."*

Pouring Out: Psalm 90:14-15 Satisfy us in the morning with your unfailing love, that we may sing for joy and be glad all our days. Make us glad for as many days as you have afflicted us, for as many years as we have seen trouble.

DAY 30

Meditation

Recognize God: *King of Kings* I Timothy 6: 15-16 God, the blessed and only Ruler, the King of kings and Lord of lords, who alone is immortal and who lives in unapproachable light, whom no one has seen or can see. To him be honor and might forever. Amen.

Recognize Jesus: *King of Kings* Revelation 17:14 They will wage war against the Lamb, but the Lamb will triumph over them because he is Lord of lords and King of kings –and with Him will be His called, chosen and faithful followers.

Worship

Adoration: I Timothy 1:17 Now to the king eternal, immortal, invisible, the only God, be honor and glory forever and ever.

Give Thanks: Jonah 2:9 But I, with shouts of grateful praise, will sacrifice to you. What I have vowed I will make good. I will say, "Salvation comes from the Lord."

"What and who am I thankful for? Thank God for them now."

Introspection

Recognize Myself: Romans 7:18b-19 For I have the desire to do what is good, but I cannot carry it out. For I do not do the good I want to do, but the evil I do not want to do – this I keep on doing.

Confession: Daniel 9:5 We have sinned and done wrong. We have been wicked and have rebelled; we have turned away from your commands and laws.

"Confess my sins here. Be specific."

How God Sees Me: I Peter 2:9 But you are a chosen people, a royal priesthood, a holy nation, God's special possession, that you may declare the praises of Him who called you out of darkness into His wonderful light.

My Call: I Timothy 6:11 But you, man of God, flee from all this, and pursue righteousness, godliness, faith, love, endurance and gentleness.

"What do I need to ask of God to carry this out in my life?"

Promise: Zephaniah 3:17 The LORD your God is with you, the Mighty Warrior who saves. He will take great delight in you; in His love He will no longer rebuke you, but will rejoice over you with singing."

*"What does this promise mean to me?
Be still and listen for God's voice."*

Pouring Out: Psalm 6:6 I am worn out from my groaning. All night long I flood my bed with weeping and drench my couch with tears.

DAY 31

Meditation

Recognize God: *Advocate* Job 16:19 Even now my witness is in heaven; my advocate is on high.

Recognize Jesus: *Advocate* I John 2:1 My dear children, I write this to you so that you will not sin. But if anybody does sin, we have an advocate with the Father – Jesus Christ, the Righteous One.

Worship

Adoration: Jude 1:25 To the only God our Savior be glory, majesty, power and authority, through Jesus Christ our Lord, before all ages, now and forevermore! Amen.

Give Thanks: Psalm 68:5-6 A father to the fatherless, a defender of widows, is God in his holy dwelling. God sets the lonely in families, he leads out the prisoners with singing; but the rebellious live in a sun-scorched land.

"What and who am I thankful for? Thank God for them now."

Introspection

Recognize Myself: James 1:14-15 But each person is tempted when they are dragged away by their own evil desire and enticed. Then after desire has conceived, it gives birth to sin; and sin, when it is full grown, gives birth to death.

Confession: Numbers 5:6-7 'Any man or woman who wrongs another in any way and so is unfaithful to the LORD is guilty and must confess the sin they have committed. They must make full restitution for the wrong they have done, add a fifth of the value to it and give it all to the persons they have wronged.'

"Confess my sins here. Be specific."

How God Sees Me: Romans 5:6 You see, at just the right time, when we were still powerless, Christ died for the ungodly.

My Call: Luke 6:31 Do to others as you would have them do to you.

"What do I need to ask of God to carry this out in my life?"

Promise: Romans 10:13 For "Everyone who calls on the name of the Lord will be saved."

*"What does this promise mean to me?
Be still and listen for God's voice."*

Pouring Out: II Chronicles 14:11 "LORD, there is no one like you to help the powerless against the mighty. Help us, LORD our God, for we rely on you, and in your name we have come against this vast army. LORD, you are our God; do not let mere mortals prevail against you.

On the next page is a prayer table. There are eight columns. The first column is for those for whom you pray for daily; usually family and close friends. The next seven are labeled with the days of the week. There all also verses to use as prompts when you pray.

Do not feel you have to fill in every blank space. The goal is not to become a praying overachiever or measuring your spirituality by the number of names on your prayer list. Your prayer life should not be a burden or a contest. The extra spaces allow room to cross names out and add new ones as circumstances change. Writing in pencil is best. This same prayer table is duplicated on the page after that so you have two copies. As time passes, you may have made so many changes that you simply need a fresh one. Ideally, you can duplicate the table on your computer and update the names on your list with ease.

The prayer tables are followed by a prayer journal where you can keep track of specific prayer requests and God's amazing answers as well as a Thanksgiving list mentioned earlier.

Your Daily Prayer List

Think carefully about this list. These are the people that are so important to you that you think about them constantly. You pray about them constantly. This will be your closest family members and friends.

Ask yourself - Who do I love? Who needs my prayers every day? Who needs my prayers without ceasing?

Your Weekly Prayer List

Your weekly prayer list is for friends, neighbors, members of your church, life group or Sunday School class; anyone who you would like to remember in prayer but don't feel you need to pray for every day. In addition to individual people, consider groups of people such as pastors, missionaries, the nation of Israel, etc. There are a lot of spaces. Squelch the desire to fill in every blank. That is not why they are there. Your lists will stretch and shrink with time and prayer – leave space for that.

At the bottom of each day is a different fruit of the Spirit to pray for within yourself. These are from Romans 5:3-5, Colossians 3:12-15 and Galatians 5:22-23.

There are so many things I ask God for. More important than my wants and needs is my walk with Christ. The more I become like Him; the more my wants and needs fade away. As you study the Word of God, you may find other godly characteristics that you would like to pray about. By all means, do!

The important thing is to pray about more than the things we want from God. Our prayers should not be "Gimme, gimme, gimme." Our goal is to be submissive to God and ask Him to mold us into what He has already planned for us.

Ephesians 2:10 declares: "For we are God's handiwork, created in Christ Jesus to do good works, which God prepared in advance for us to do.

Daily & Weekly Prayer List

Daily	Sunday	Monday	Tuesday
II Timothy 4:18 Deliver me from every evil attack	Eph.3:16 May He Strengthen you w/ power thru His Spirt	Eph. 4:2 Bear with one another in love	Matthew 6:33 Seek first the Kingdom of God
Family	Pastors/ My Church	Caregivers / Shut-Ins	Our nation / leaders
Fruit of Spirit: Love, Wisdom	Fruit of Spirit: Perseverance	Fruit of Spirit: Faithfulness	Fruit of Spirit: Hope

Daily & Weekly Prayer List			
Wednesday Philippians 4:19 My God will supply every need	**Thursday** Rom. 10:1 ...That they be saved.	**Friday** Col.4:3 May God open a door for our message.	**Saturday** I Cor. 1:10 Agree w/ one another & be united
Widows / Widowers	Persecuted Christians	Missionaries	My friends / neighbors
Fruit of Spirit: Kindness	*Fruit of Spirit: Patience*	*Fruit of Spirit: Self Control*	*Fruit of Spirit: Forgiving*

Daily & Weekly Prayer List			
Daily II Timothy 4:18 Deliver me from every evil attack	**Sunday** Eph.3:16 May He Strengthen you w/ power thru His Spirt	**Monday** Eph. 4:2 Bear with one another in love	**Tuesday** Matthew 6:33 Seek first the Kingdom of God
Family	Pastors/ My Church	Caregivers / Shut-Ins	Our nation / leaders
Fruit of Spirit: *Love, Wisdom*	*Fruit of Spirit:* *Perseverance*	*Fruit of Spirit:* *Faithfulness*	*Fruit of Spirit:* *Hope*

Daily & Weekly Prayer List

Wednesday	Thursday	Friday	Saturday
Philippians 4:19 My God will supply every need	Rom. 10:1 ...That they be saved.	Col. 4:3 May God open a door for our message.	I Cor. 1:10 Agree w/ one another & be united
Widows / Widowers	Persecuted Christians	Missionaries	My friends / neighbors
Fruit of Spirit: Kindness	*Fruit of Spirit: Patience*	*Fruit of Spirit: Self Control*	*Fruit of Spirit: Forgiving*

Prayer Journal

Keep track of your prayer requests and God's answers here.

DATE	NAME

PRAYER REQUEST	ANSWER & DATE

DATE	NAME

PRAYER REQUEST	ANSWER & DATE

My THANKSGIVING LIST

My THANKSGIVING LIST

My friend. I am honored that you chose to read my book. I am praying for each person who holds this book in their hands. I hope that through it, you will draw close to our Heavenly Father and find your prayer life revitalized.

Other Books by Terri Blazell-Wayson

Lisa's Testimony: A Dog's Walk through the 23rd Psalm

Join Lisa as she shares in her journey of faith and trust in both her master and her "Master Creator."

Christopher's Story: A Dog's Walk through John 3:16

Christopher lets his nose guide him as he tells the story of his life from the first time he met his broken, human family to when he must say good bye. Along the way, he weaves the beauty of John 3:16 and the love of God through their tender story.

Words for Women Who Hurt

Words for Women Who Hurt spills off the pages with a message of hope and healing to those who are hurt and broken.

Words for Women Who Hurt Small Group Study Guide

This study guide digs deeper into the "sisterhood" of women in the Bible such as Rahab, Abigail, Tamar and adds another layer of hope and understand to each woman's story.

Three Desperate Women

Society considers them worthless and outcasts. Each has an encounter with Jesus and everything changes.

www.ingramcontent.com/pod-product-compliance
Lightning Source LLC
Chambersburg PA
CBHW060344050426
42449CB00011B/2821